Learning from the Pulp Masters

Lessons from Prolific Authors

Dr. Robert C. Worstell, editor

While every precaution has been taken in the preparation of this book, the publisher assumes no responsibility for errors or omissions, or for damages resulting from the use of the information contained herein.

LEARNING FROM THE PULP MASTERS: 2ND EDITION

First edition. February 17, 2019.

Copyright © 2019 Dr. Robert C. Worstell.

ISBN: 979-8201116934

Written by Dr. Robert C. Worstell.

Table of Contents

To all our many devoted and loyal fans -

We write and publish these stories <u>only</u> for you.

(Be sure to get your bonuses at the end of this book...)

Introduction

THIS IS JUST ANOTHER compilation of notes I had left over from research. Cutting-room floor pieces.

I got into studying the pulp-magazine era authors with Lester Dent while I was studying the conventional wisdom of 'plotting".

The last find, of H. Bedford-Jones' "This Fiction Business" is so conclusive that very little else is needed. There, he tells the variety of issues that authors of his day encountered.

This book is a companion piece to that book and so doesn't need to repeat any of his jocular description of how he made a very good living writing and selling stories during that age.

I have included two chapters of Bedford-Jones' short book here – just so you can get a simple overview along with these other authors.

Good luck with your studies.

Robert C. Worstell

William Wallace Cook

From "The Fiction Factory"

NICKEL THRILLS AND DOLLAR SHOCKERS.

THE WORD "SENSATIONAL" as applied to fiction has been burdened with an opprobrium which does not rightfully belong to it. Ignorance and prejudice and hypocrisy have conspired to defame a very worthy word.

Certain good but misguided people will turn shudderingly from a nickel novel and complacently look for thrills in a "best seller." Often and often the "best seller" is to be had for 95 cents or $1 at the department stores. Not infrequently it spills more blood than the nickel thriller, but the blood is spilled on finer paper, and along with it are idealized pictures of heroine and hero done by the best artists.

As a matter of course the dollar dreadful is better done. The author probably took six months or a year to do it, and if it is well advertised and proves a success he reaps a modest fortune. On the other hand, the nickel novel is written in three days or a week and brings the author $50. Why shouldn't the dollar book show a higher grade of craftmanship? But is it less vicious than the novel that sells for five cents? To draw the matter still finer, is either form of fiction vicious?

If we turn to Webster and seek a definition of "sensational" we find: "Suited or intended to excite temporarily great interest or emotion; melodramatic; emotional."

This does not mean that sensational writing is vicious writing. It is wrong to classify as vicious or degrading the story of swift action and clean ethics, or to compare it with that prurient product of the slums which deals with problems of sex.

The tale that moves breathlessly but logically, that is built incident upon incident to a telling climax with the frankly avowed purpose to entertain, that has no questionable leanings or immoral affiliations—such a tale speeds innocently an idle hour, diverts pleasantly the harrassed mind, freshens our zeal for the duties of life, and occasionally leaves us with higher ideals.

We are all dreamers. We must be dreamers before we are doers. If some of the visions that come to us in secret reverie were flaunted in all their conceit and inconsistency before the world, not one of us but would be the butt of the world's ridicule. And yet, out of these highly tinted imaginings springs the impulse that carries us to higher and nobler things.

A difference in the price of two commodities does not necessarily mark a moral difference in the commodities themselves. The Century Magazine sells for 35 cents, while The Argosy sells for 10 cents. You will be told that The Century is "high class" and with a distinct literary flavor, perhaps that it is more elevating. Even so; yet which of these magazines is doing more to make the world really livable? Ask the newsdealer in your town how many Centuries he sells, and how many Argosies.

Readers are not made for the popular magazines, but the popular magazines are made for the people. Unless there was a distinct and insistent demand for this sort of entertainment, so many all-story magazines, priced at a dime, could not exist.

....

The life of today sets a pattern for the fiction of to-day. The masses demand rapid-fire action and good red brawn in their reading matter. Their awakened moral sense makes possible the muck-raker; and when they weary of the day's evil and the day's toil, it is their habit to divert themselves with pleasant and exciting reading. And it must be CLEAN.

WHEN FICTION IS STRANGER THAN TRUTH

WE ARE TOLD THAT "FICTION hath in it a higher end than fact," which we may readily believe; and we may also concede that "truth is stranger than fiction," at least in its occasional application. Nevertheless, in the course of his career as a writer Edwards has created two fictional fancies which so closely approximated truth as to make fiction stranger than truth; and, in one case, the net result of imagination was to coincide exactly with real facts of which the imagination could take no account. Perhaps each of these two instances is unique in its particular field; they are, in any event, so odd as to be worthy of note.

In the early 90's, when a great deal of Edwards' work was appearing, unsigned, in The Detroit Free Press, he wrote for that paper a brief sketch entitled, "The Fatal Hand." The sketch was substantially as follows:

"The Northern Pacific Railroad had just been built into Helena, Montana, and I happened to be in the town one evening and stepped into a gambling hall. Burton, a friend of mine, was playing poker with a miner and two professional gamblers. I stopped beside the table and watched the game.

Cards had just been drawn. Burton, as soon as he had looked at his hand, calmly shoved the cards together, laid them face-downward in front of him, removed a notebook from his pocket and scribbled something on a blank leaf. 'Read that,' said he, 'when you get back to your hotel tonight.'

The play proceeded. Presently the miner detected one of the professional gamblers in the act of cheating. Words were passed, the lie given. All the players leaped to their feet. Burton, in attempting to keep the miner from shooting, received the gambler's bullet and fell dead upon the scattered cards.

An hour later, when I reached my hotel, I thought of the note Burton had handed me. It read: 'I have drawn two red sevens. I now hold jacks full on red sevens. It is a fatal hand and I shall never leave this table alive. I have $6,000 in the First National Bank at Bismarck. Notify my mother, Mrs. Ezra J. Burton, Louisville, Kentucky.'"

This small product of the Fiction Factory was pure fiction from beginning to end. In the original it had the tang of point and counterpoint which caused it to be seized upon by other papers and widely copied. This gave extensive publicity to the "fatal hand"—the three jacks and two red sevens contrived by Edwards out of a small knowledge of poker and the cabala of cards.

Yet, what was the result?

A month later the Chicago papers published an account of a police raid on a gambling room. As the officers rushed into the place a man at one of the tables fell forward and breathed his last. "Heart disease," was the verdict. But note: A police officer looked at the cards the dead man had held and found them to be three jacks and two red sevens.

A week later The New York Recorder gave space to a news story in which a man was slain at a gaming table in Texas. When the smoke of the shooting had blown away some one made the discovery that he had held the fatal hand.

From that time on for several months the fatal hand left a trail of superstition and gore all over the West. How many murders and hopeless attacks of heart failure it was responsible for Edwards had no means of knowing, but he could scarcely pick up a paper without finding an account of some of the ravages caused by his "jacks full on red sevens."

Query: Were the reporters of the country romancing? If not, will some psychologist kindly rise and explain how a bit of fiction could be responsible for so much real tragedy?

LOVE YOUR WORK FOR THE WORK'S SAKE

BEFORE A YOUNG MAN throws himself into the ranks of this vast army of writers, let him ponder the situation well. If, under the iron heel of adversity, he is sure he can still love his work for the work's sake and be true to himself, there is one chance in ten that he will make a fair living, and one chance in a hundred that he may become one of the generals.

The sentiment which Edwards has tried to carry through every paragraph and line of this book is this, that "Writing is its own reward." His meaning is, that to the writer the joy of the work is something infinitely higher, finer and more satisfying than its pecuniary value to the editor who buys it. Material success, of course, is a necessity, unless—happy condition!—the writer has a private income on which to draw for meeting the sordid demands of life. But this also is true: A writer even of modest talent will have material success in a direct ratio with the joy he finds in his work!—Because, brother of the pen, when one takes pleasure in an effort, then that effort attracts merit inevitably. If any writing is a merciless grind the result will show it—and the editor will see it, and reject.

There are times, however, when doubt shakes the firmest confidence. A writer will have moods into which will creep a distrust of the work upon which he is at that moment engaged. If necessity spurs him on and he cannot rise above his misgivings, the story will testify to the lack of faith, doubts will increase as defects multiply and the story will be ruined. THE WRITER MUST HAVE FAITH IN HIS WORK QUITE APART FROM THE MONEY HE EXPECTS TO RECEIVE FOR IT. If he has this faith he reaches toward a spiritual success beside which the highest material success is paltry indeed.

When a writer sits down to a story let him blind his eyes to the financial returns, even though they may be sorely needed. Let him forget that his wares are to be offered for sale, and consider them as being wrought for his own diversion. Let him say to himself, "I shall make this the best story I have ever written; I shall weave my soul into its warp and whether it sells or not I shall be satisfied to know that I have put upon paper the BEST that is in me." If he will do this, he will achieve a spiritual success and—as surely as day follows night—a material success beyond his fondest dreams. BUT he must keep his eye single to the TRUE success and must have no commerce in thought with what may come to him materially.

To some, all this may appear too idealistic, too transcendental. There are natures so worldly, perhaps even among writers, as to scoff at the idea of spiritual success. They are overshadowed by the Material, and when the Spiritual, which is the true source of their power, is no longer the "still, small voice" of their inspiration, they will be bankrupt materially as well.

A writer cannot hide himself in his work. His individuality is written into it, and he may be read between the lines for what he is. A creation reflects the creator, and that the work may be good the writer should have spiritual ideals and do his utmost to live up to them. Let him have a purpose, be it never so humble, to benefit in some way his fellow-man, and let him hew steadily to the line. Love your work for the work's sake and material benefits "will be added unto you."

From "The Complete Plotto"

THEME. EVERY STORY has a Theme, or an underlying proposition that indicates its type. The Theme may be clear-cut and distinct, or shadowy and vague; it is always in evidence, and differentiates one type of story from all the other types. Around each Theme any number of distinctly different stories may be written.

A story may be constructed with, or without, a certain Theme in mind. Rarely perhaps does a writer begin a story with a set Theme in front of him. He may develop his plot from a situation, or Conflict; nevertheless, as the plot develops the Theme develops with it. The writer will feel the Theme and, consciously or unconsciously, combine his Conflicts to a certain pattern. This pattern, plain in the finished work, will conform to a Theme.

. . . .

THE CONFLICTS. Desire, in some one of its many forms, is responsible for the awakening of Purpose. Something from without, impinging upon something within, excites a feeling or an emotion, and the soul flows into Purpose, and Purpose into action. Then, somewhere on the path of rising action. Purpose encounters Obstacle. At this point, and at this point only, do we establish what writers of creative fiction call a situation. Purpose alone never made a situation; Obstacle alone never made one; but strike the flint of Obstacle with the steel of Purpose and sparks of situation begin to fly.

...[A] Method of plot suggestion for writers of creative fiction, is founded upon this law: Purpose, expressed or implied, opposing Obstacle, expressed or implied, yields Conflict.

PURPOSES AND OBSTACLES, How many Purposes are there in the world? Not many, although their variations are infinite. Perhaps, in the last analysis one General Purpose would comprehend all the Purposes: TO ACHIEVE HAPPINESS. That is the end and aim of life on this planet. But happiness has a different meaning for most of us. There is the happiness of love and courtship, of married life, of achieving wealth or power by all the many methods, good or evil, that may be contrived by the thinking mind. Religion may be the road to happiness for some, and revenge the road to a doubtful happiness for others. The virtues or the faults of a human soul set the pattern of Purpose for that soul.

Plotto concerns itself with but one General Purpose in its application to three general goals of endeavor:

1. To Achieve Happiness in Love and Courtship.

2. To Achieve Happiness in Married Life.

3. To Achieve Happiness (Success) in Enterprise.

Yet, while this one General Purpose runs through all the Conflicts, a host of subordinate Purposes will appear in them, opposed by an infinite number of Obstacles.

There is one Supreme Purpose in every life: TO LIVE; and there is one Supreme Obstacle each life encounters: DEATH. Complicating the scheme and giving zest to the plot of life are innumerable subordinate Purposes and Obstacles, dealing with all the enterprises of which life is capable.

Overshadowed by the Supreme Purpose of LIFE, and the Supreme Obstacle of DEATH, we wage our mimic wars of conquest and gain; but, at any minute, the Supreme Purpose may fail, and Death come striding into our finite calculations and calling a truce. There is also a Paramount Purpose in all the lesser activities of our existence, opposed by a Paramount Obstacle; and they marshal their secondary Purposes and Obstacles to keep us "on our toes" and fighting valiantly for all we have, or hope to have. Blessed be Purpose! And thrice-blessed be Obstacle!

The Conflicts in Plotto are brief statements of Purpose in active opposition with Obstacle—situations which are to be combined with other situations. For instance: "A, in love with B, is not favored by F-B, father of B." Here is the implied Purpose, "To Achieve Happiness in Love," meeting an Obstacle bluntly expressed.

Purpose and Obstacle give concrete exemplification of the Theme in every form of fictional narrative, whether short story, novelette, or novel.

THE SHORT STORY. Purpose and Obstacle at grips in one dramatic situation will define the short story, since it is calculated to leave a single dominant impression upon the reader's mind. Ordinarily, this form of narrative fiction will be woven about a plot of the simplest construction. There will be the main situation as suggested by a chosen Conflict, the Conflict leading up to it and the Conflict carrying on and terminating the action. These three Conflicts may be reduced to two, if the main Conflict should in itself possess the qualities of a terminal Conflict. Conflicts too long, or too involved, for short story purposes will usually be found to be broken Conflicts. When such a Conflict is selected for the main situation, it is possible to use only that part of it which contains the most dramatic appeal.

THE NOVELETTE. This form of narrative fiction may be considered as a long short story, or as a short novel. If the former, the Conflict suggesting the situation will be elaborated with dramatic material concerned with the Purpose and Obstacle. If, on the other hand, the novelette partakes of the character of a short novel, the Paramount Purpose and Obstacle will involve subordinate Purposes and Obstacles all cumulative in power and bearing upon the story's climax or crisis. Here, as everywhere, the imagination must exercise constructive judgment.

THE NOVEL. The full-fledged novel may be considered as consisting of several short stories all leading up to, and intimately bound up with, the Paramount Purpose and Obstacle that give the complete story its unity. Construction here plays its most discriminating role, for the subordinate situations must grow toward a single, decisive crisis. The effect must be cumulative. If the main Conflict shall involve the crisis—and it should—all the subordinate situations dealing with the Theme will be so selected as to grow naturally in dramatic strength toward the climax. Here no rules of construction will take the place of taste and discrimination. The constructive imagination, properly exercised, will deal capably with the situations, and the creative imagination will work a miracle of dramaturgic power.

ORIGINALITY. The Conflicts all come from the vast storehouse of Human Nature. They are there, millions upon millions of them, waiting for the imagination to select them and group them in an original combination. For there is "nothing new under the sun." Originality in creative work comes from our own individual use of the tools so bountifully provided by the Divine Creator. All that is possible to a mortal craftsman is the combining of old material into something new and different.

Originality is the ideal of the Plotto Method; and it is realized by disregarding the references prefixed and affixed to the Conflicts and (or) interpreting the Specific as well as the General, Conflicts in terms of the Plottoist's own experience. Nothing in the Specific Conflicts will be used literally, but the concrete exemplification in such Conflicts will serve as a suggestion, lending wings to the creative imagination for its own high flight.

For original combinations of Conflicts the Classification by Symbols will be found a treasure-trove of suggestions. If the main Conflict selected is built around A, or B, alone, the A or B group should be scanned; if around A and B alone, the A and B group will yield suggestions, or the A or B group may be found to serve; or, if several characters are involved in the main Conflict, reference may be had to that particular group of symbols. If a certain group of symbols proves too limited, drop one of the lesser character symbols and consult the group represented by those remaining. This course may be followed, in the search for original combinations, until only the protagonist remains in the situation. Somewhere along the line of search the imagination is certain to find exactly what it is looking for.

Erle Stanley Gardner

FROM *Secrets of the World's Best-Selling Writer*

By Francis L. and Roberta B. Fugate

Note: except from where Gardner is referred to in the third person by the Fugates, these quotes are from Gardner's archives.

Work on every plot until you have

> 1. Unusual opening incident
>
> 2. Complete character conflicts
>
> 3. Some emotional appeal
>
> 4. Some unusual slant of characters and situation
>
> 5. All stock situations eliminated

. . . .

The pulp writer's insurance policy: continuing characters.

. . . .

Make a genuine reader suspense in which he doesn't know what will happen next and is surprised either by

> (a) What does happen
>
> (b) The way in which it happens

. . . .

My own approach to the question is different from that of the critic. I am a writer. I serve the reading public. The reading public is my master.

. . . .

Every story, or rather, every type of story that has succeeded has the common point of a single man, unaided, overcoming difficulties by the inherent power that is within him and attached to him. The western story gets by because the cowpuncher depends only on his gun for his law and order, for his safety. He is apart from the machine, away from the routine. The air story shows a pilot up in the air, away from civilization, fighting. The crook story shows a lone wolf fighting the law. The detective story features a hero who stands apart from the forces of law and order as represented by the cops, and fights his own battles against the crooks.

. . . .

In my opinion a good plot never hops into a person's mind. Nor do I believe it is possible for a person to sit down and think up a plot. I know I can't do it.

A plot has to be built.

If we know the necessary ingredients which go into a plot we can start taking those ingredients and fitting them together one at a time. If we are sure of the stability of our building blocks we know that by the time we get done putting them together we are going to have a structure. It may not be the structure we want but it is enough of a structure so that we can start remodeling here and there and get the type of structure we want.

The first thing we need in connection with any story is a story situation which appeals to the public.

The public wants stories because it wants to escape. We talk about escape literature, yet we don't stop to think of how we escape by the use of escape literature, what we escape from, and why there is this yearning for escape.

Writing stories is a great profession and to be able to write interesting stories is a great privilege. The writer is bringing moral strength to many millions of people because the successful story inspires the audience.

If a story doesn't inspire an audience in some way, it is no good.

Any story which really inspires an audience has some basic appeal and for want of a better term I have assembled some of these and called them the lowest common denominator of public interest.

Every successful story, and above all every successful character, has as his very foundation one or more of these lowest common denominators of public interest. Therefore whenever a writer reads a story or sees a character that appeals to him he should start looking for the lowest common denominator of public interest which is in that story or in that character and which has appealed to the public.

There are three major characters who have been virtually indestructible in the course of fiction: Robin Hood, Sherlock Holmes and Cinderella.

Bear in mind that it is not always easy to determine exactly what is the lowest common denominator of public interest. It is quite possible that the person will think he has it but find out that he doesn't have it. Therefore, as far as possible, the person should never try to get the interest germ or kernel out of one story or out of one character and think he has found the lowest common denominator. He must find something which appears in almost every story that appeals to the public. Sometimes it is one denominator, sometimes another, but there probably are very few of these really lowest common denominators of public interest.

. . . .

However, if we want to find the real basis for popularity I think we need to look at the advertising of the day.

The advertiser pays a lot of money for writing. He isn't paid for writing, he pays for writing. He has to buy the space in which he puts his copy and of necessity that copy must be good enough to bring in returns which more than justify the cost of the space. Therefore whenever we find any basic trend in advertising we can be certain that it is paying off, and if advertising is paying off it is paying off because it is getting public response. And if it gets a public response it is because it has touched a responsive chord in the minds of the public. Therefore by watching advertising we can get a pretty good idea of certain common denominators of public interest.

Sometime ago one of the advertisers started the idea of self-improvement without work: Play the piano in six easy lessons, "Imagine their surprise when I answered the waiter in French." The girl who got engaged wasn't the one with the charming personality and the good figure but the girl who washed her face with Woodbury's Facial Soap. The man who dominated the directors' meeting had been given Sanka Coffee the night before. The life of the party, with a wealth of information, was one who had had the foresight to subscribe to Elbert Hubbard's Scrapbook, and so on, down the line.

This trend of advertising is alarming, but it can't be discounted. It represents a growing trend on the part of the public to get something for nothing and to acquire culture while drinking Sanka Coffee or beauty while rubbing the lather of Woodbury's Facial Soap on the skin.

Sherlock Holmes had this common denominator of public interest and I think it is the big factor in the Holmes stories.

The reader identified himself with Sherlock Holmes to such an extent that Holmes' mental feats of observation and deduction appeared so easy the reader became convinced that he could go out and duplicate the processes. At least for a time, the reader thought he could fly and had the sense of power which went with it.

The Cinderella story has been told and retold many, many thousands of times. It is a common denominator which has the greatest public appeal. It is a soothing syrup to the unfortunate. It leads people to believe that there is somewhere a magic power, a fairy godmother, which will make their dreams come true—therefore it isn't simply a waste of time to have dreams. People love to dream, people love to yearn. If they can be convinced that the yearning and the dreaming have some solid foundation in fact they are going to love the media by which that belief is inculcated in their minds.

There are various modifications of the Cinderella story.

How many times have we seen in pictures the story of the young woman who wore her hair slicked back, had unsightly spectacles, dressed in a dumpy manner, and lost out or all but lost out to a female vamp who had curves and wiggles? Then suddenly there was a transformation. The girl got the right idea. She had her hair fluffed out, she put on spectacles which didn't show or used contact lenses, and became the ravishing beauty.

These things have a basic foundation in the human mind. The girl who is ugly yearns to be beautiful. If she is convinced that perhaps she can become beautiful she has received a terrific lift. It has helped her character. It has helped her master the problems of life.

There are many of these common denominators of public interest and yet probably fifteen or twenty of them would cover the whole gamut of successful story writing.

The point is that a writer in starting a story should first decide what lowest common denominator of public interest, or what combination of common denominators he is going to put in the story. Once he puts them in the story he knows he is starting on a firm foundation. If he doesn't have them in the story he doesn't have anything.

. . . .

The only way to make an audience take a real interest in a person is to present a likable person in a sympathetic manner. The audience first has to know that person. Therefore, it seems to me that in creating a Mason show on television one of the first things to do is to start with some character who is to become Perry Mason's client and to make the audience like that character. And of course since the story is a Perry Mason story and we have to switch to Perry Mason so early in the story, we have to do some fast writing in order to get the attention of the audience, the interest of the audience, and the affection of the audience so that by the time events threaten to engulf this character and Mason enters the picture the audience is inclined to cheer.

This is the same lowest common denominator of public interest which on a physical plane was manifested by the beautiful woman kidnapped by the redskins and about to be taken off to a life of shame and torture when someone would summon the United States Cavalry and we would see the Cavalry galloping shoulder to shoulder, with the flag waving and the horses pounding over the road.

Everyone wanted to get up and cheer.

Mason has to do the thing mentally which the Cavalry did physically.

Therefore when I see these scripts come in where the first characters are disagreeable, where there is slapping and physical violence and it is hard to become interested in any particular character, then we see a crime committed and know that Mason is expected to solve that crime, I feel that we are selling our character down the river. I want to vomit at the idea of the great Perry Mason with his sense of justice, his basic faith in human nature, descending so low as to be hired to represent a person of that caliber.

In short, it seems to me that we can say to all writers that it is a basic rule of the Perry Mason stories that the audience must want the character to be represented by Perry Mason to come out on top.

If this is done too obviously we simply burlesque the whole situation. It must be done in a subtle manner.

The Mason stories are stories of mystery. It seems to me that in addition to a lovable character we should start with something in the line of a mystery which intrigues the audience.

. . . .

My definition of a mystery is that it consists of a series of interesting events which have sinister implications and the logic of which cannot be instantly comprehended by the audience.

Therefore it seems almost essential to me that we should open our stories with some event which attracts the interest of the audience, which seems to have somewhat sinister overtones because they know they are going to be watching a murder mystery, and which simply intrigues the hell out of the audience.

Obviously, getting such a situation is not an easy matter and if we try to conjure one up without knowing the basic rules pertaining to such a situation we are simply wearying our minds by trying to climb a mental greased pole.

There are however certain basic laws for getting such a situation and once we understand those laws we can build the situation into our story just as we can start with a common denominator of public interest and build that into the story.

In a mystery story the opening situation can best be understood by referring to what I have called the murderer's ladder.

Understand that it is not always necessary for the audience to see every step in this ladder but the writer should have each step in mind when he starts to think about the murder. He should know the motivation for the murder, he should understand the temptation, he should know the over-all plan.

However, the basic story situation comes when the murderer starts to climb from the rung of the ladder which represents the first action which can't be withdrawn. In other words, at a certain point the murderer has committed himself; he has started his action; he has broken into the house where he intends to commit the murder; he has surreptitiously boarded the yacht where his victim is sleeping; he has put the poison in the glass. He has done something which he isn't supposed to do and which, if detected, will expose the fact that he has murder in his mind. It is the point where he can't back up. In the motivation of murder it is the point of no return.

Once the murderer reaches this point it is only necessary to provide some event which makes his plans go awry in order to bring about a story situation. The murderer can't back up. He has to go forward. His plans have been knocked into a cocked hat. Therefore he has to improvise. He starts improvising with an image of the hangman's rope dangling over his neck. He has to improvise in a hurry. There is this terrific element of urgency which is crowding him.

Therefore he does something which brings about a sufficiently paradoxical situation as far as the audience is concerned, knowing only what it knows at that time, so that the audience is intrigued and sees a pattern of interesting or perhaps exciting events taking place with the unmistakable background of urgency, yet those are events which puzzle the audience, which arouse its interest and moves breathlessly but logically, that is built incident upon incident to a telling climax with the frankly avowed purpose to entertain, that has no questionable leanings or immoral affiliations—such a tale speeds innocently an idle hour, diverts pleasantly the harassed mind, freshens our zeal for the duties of life, and occasionally leaves us with higher ideals, which bring about an atmosphere of mystery.

. . . .

A book of this sort may be used in various ways. A writer should have a constructive mind. If he uses any mechanical plot help to do his thinking for him his stories are going to be weak. If he uses a plot device to help get his imagination working, he's saving himself time and trouble. In my own case I used Plotto to find out what a plot was and how to build it. I secured data from it which has been worth a great deal to me. I think any book is of greater or lesser value, depending upon how it is used. I don't think the author ever intended Plotto to be used by a writer as a substitute for thought. I always figured his illustrations were just illustrations and that the author who wanted to build plots from the Plotto method should have what I call "imaginative equivalents." Deeper than all this, however, lies a mine of pure gold in this book.

. . . .

Unless you are deliberately creating a superman type, which distinctly appeals to the juvenile mind, the reader loses sympathy with a character who becomes too invincible. A reader likes to identify himself with the central character. A reader always feels that when he's really in training he can smash some guy on the kisser and make him stay down. He feels this, even when he is fat, fifty, and out of condition.

. . . .

The real definition of a character is one who stands out from the common run of mankind.

. . . .

Gardner developed his most comprehensive and reliable plotting system from the theory that certain activities and appetites are basic human motivations: desire for sex, wealth, travel, human friendship and contact, food, self-improvement (mental, physical, financial), security, advancement, and justice. In life, each desire is confronted by conflicts—personal, circumstantial, and financial obstacles. The person with a desire attempts to overcome conflicts by a counterattack, a detour, or flight. This is the real-life workings of William Wallace Cook's law: "Purpose, expressed or implied, opposing Obstacle, expressed or implied, yields Conflict"—the basis of all story construction.

. . . .

Gardner developed "The Fluid or Unstatic Theory of Plots" over a period of several years and many revisions as an aid to keeping a story in constant forward dramatic motion from that first incidental mystery which challenges the interest of the reader to the final "blow-off" when the protagonist solves the case in a blaze of action. In constructing a plot, the author worked through nine steps:

1. The act of primary villainy

2. Motivation for act of villainy

3. The villain's cover-up

4. Complications which arise during and after the cover-up

5. The hero's contact with the act of villainy

6. Further complications and character conflicts

7. Suspense through hero's mistakes

8. Villain's further attempts to escape

9. Hero sets solution factors in motion or traps villain

. . . .

Life is so complex that events are always impinging upon individuals. It is human nature to see only one's own life and the events which comprise it. But the events which comprise the life of any one individual are, in turn, the results of causes in the lives of others. Therefore, if we take three old, hackneyed plots—which are old and hackneyed because they are true to life—and start them revolving in separate groups, affecting three separate groups of individuals, and then take the place where those plots impinge upon a common ground and use the results of that impinging contact for motivation for a main plot we have something on which to work...

. . . .

All plots are old. The attempt to get a novel plot is what makes for strained story construction. . . . it's the piecing together of the different story characters into a new series of interlocking events which gives an appearance of freshness to an otherwise devitalized plot.

The Scott Meredith /Algis Budrys' Plot Skeleton

I'M POSTING THIS HERE as research notes so that anyone can find what I took hours to dig up.

The reason we want to study formulas and "skeletons" is to train our unconscious mind better on what we need in order to crank out decent, salable genre fiction. Once you have this internalized, then your stories will flow more simply.

Scott Meredith (not the author) was an agent who got his claim to fame in finding authors for the pulp fiction magazines. He developed a nice scam of getting newbie authors to pay him to read their stories. He then hired others (James Blish was one of them) to write rejection letters to them, giving "helpful" advice about how to improve their stories. Those writers got about a tenth of the money paid and were paid by their production. Those writers were expected to read (at least skim) the book. His agency is still working today, although I doubt they use this "reading system" any longer.

I ran into DW Smith crediting Meredith for a "plot skeleton", which had seven points. Unfortunately, and as you'll see, the versions run from four to five to seven. Aldis Budrys' plot skeleton that he teaches today is closest to what Smith teaches. I haven't found the Budrys/Meredith connection (yet.)

My notes:

Creators of Science Fiction – Brian Stableford, pg 112

"...commonly-quoted versions still to the original four: a sympathetic protagonist; an urgent problem; complications caused by initial failure to solve the problem; and a solution by means of the protagonist's heroic efforts."

The Science of Science-fiction Writing – James E. Gunn, pg 19

"Damon Knight, however, worked for Scott Meredith and includes what he calls 'the plot skeleton' in his Writer's Digest book "Creating Short Fiction." I offer it below:

1. a believable and sympathetic central character;

2. his urgent and difficult problem;

3. his attempts to resolve the problem, which fail and make his situation more desperate;

4. the crisis, his last chance to win;

5. the successful resolution, brought about by means of the central character's own courage, ingenuity, etc.

Knight continues: 'The reverse of this plot is the story in which the central character is the villain; the story ends with his defeat rather than with his victory.'"

The Sociology of Science Fiction – Brian M. Stableford, pg 39

"1. A sympathetic and believable lead character;

2. an urgent and vital problem;

3. complications caused by the lead character's unsuccessful attempts to solve the problem;

4. the crisis;

5. the resolution, in which the lead character solves the problem by means of his own courage and resourcefulness."

The Seven Point Plot Skeleton

(FROM: SFFCHRONICLES.com/threads/10092)

The Seven Point Plot came up in another thread, where it elicited some interest and questions. I just knew I had it filed away somewhere, and since Kathy has a fair few questions to wade through before she'll have the time to explain it further, I finally summoned up the energy for a search through my files.

And, in fact, I found three different versions.

The first one seems to be attributed to the late Scott Meredith, a very high- profile literary agent in his time, but there is a question mark after his name, and I have no idea why I put it there. So here is what Scott Meredith (or someone) had to say:

a protagonist (1) has a problem (2) and endeavors to solve it (3) but meets with difficulties (4) whereupon he learns something (5) which enables him to make another attempt (6)

leading to a resolution (7)

The second version is from Algis Budrys (and is probably the one recommended here by K. D. Wentworth):

(1) a character (2) in context (3) with a problem

(4)which the character tries to solve (5) only to experience unexpected failure (6) followed by either victory or defeat, leaving a need for (7) validation

Version number three is entitled "The Seven Basic Steps of Human Action" by John Truby (according to a quick search at Google, he teaches screen-writing):

1) a problem or need affecting the hero

2) desire (what the hero wants)

3) an opponent (someone competing for the same goal as the protagonist)

4) a plan (for overcoming the opponent and achieving success)

5) battle (a final conflict which determines which of them attains the goal

6) self-revelation (a fundamental understanding the hero gains, which in some way fulfills the original need)

7) a new equilibrium (the conflict resolved, the world goes on, but with the hero at a higher or lower point than before)

Science-fiction Studies, Vol 18, Issue 1, page 38

"The most succinct statement of the Scott Meredith Plot Skeleton I've yet seen is Damon Knight's 'You gotta have a hero, and the hero's gotta win.'"

Phillip Brewer

(HTTPS://WWW.PHILIPBREWER.net/story-structure-in-short-stories/)

One good model for story structure (taught to me by Bruce Holland Rogers) is Algis Budrys's seven point story structure. It has:

1. a character,
2. in a situation,
3. with a problem,
4. who tries repeatedly to solve his problem,
5. but repeatedly fails, (usually making the problem worse),
6. then, at the climax of the story, makes a final attempt (which might either succeed or fail, depending on the kind of story it is), after which
7. the result is "validated" in a way that makes it clear that what we saw was, in fact, the final result.

Another good one (taught to me by Steven Barnes) is Joseph Campbell's Hero's Journey:

1. The hero is confronted with a challenge,
2. rejects it,
3. but then is forced (or allowed) to accept it.

4. He travels on the road of trials,
5. gathering powers and allies, and
6. confronts evil—only to be defeated.
7. This leads to a dark night of the soul, after which
8. the hero makes a leap of faith that allows him to confront evil again and be victorious.
9. Finally, the student becomes the teacher.

Flash Fiction Online

(HTTP://WWW.FLASHFICTIONONLINE.com/c20100202-how-low-can-you-go-bruce-holland-rogers.html)

Bruce Holland Rogers guest posting:

> *"(T)he theory first described by Scott Meredith and later taught by Algis Budrys, (goes) something like this: A character in a context has a problem that she tries three time(s) to solve, failing each time, at which point the character either has an insight, changes her approach, and succeeds or refuses the insight, tries the same thing she has tried before, and is destroyed."*

This last description aligns Campbell with Lester Dent, and makes it possible to write short stories with the whole Heroes Journey in it.

DW Smith credits mostly Scott Meredith, but you'll see that he actually uses Aldis Budrys in his courses.

Compared to Lester Dent Model, All Together Now...

YOU HAVE TO ALSO COMPARE this to the Lester Dent model. The seven-points are there, with the character-setting-problem in the first section, then three try-fails, with the third winding up as the crisis and resolution. Budreys' use of the "validation" is given more emphasis by Smith as a way to end stories. You are essentially telling a person that it's OK to close the book now.

You now can start to see how Budrys, Dent, and Campbell all align. Dent has three try-fails, as does Campbell, and the last one becoming the climax. During the above, you can see an evolution of the main character having to evolve (learn) through the story.

This is why beginning authors should study plotting until it is coming out of their ears – and then throw it all away. Use what works for you and your readers most appreciate. You'll be able to tell by the sales.

Lester Dent

The Lester Dent Pulp Paper Master Fiction Plot

BY LESTER DENT

This is a formula, a master plot, for any 6000 word pulp story. It has worked on adventure, detective, western and war-air. It tells exactly where to put everything. It shows definitely just what must happen in each successive thousand words.

No yarn of mine written to the formula has yet failed to sell.

The business of building stories seems not much different from the business of building anything else.

Here's how it starts:

1. A DIFFERENT MURDER METHOD FOR VILLAIN TO USE

2. A DIFFERENT THING FOR VILLAIN TO BE SEEKING

3. A DIFFERENT LOCALE

4. A MENACE WHICH IS TO HANG LIKE A CLOUD OVER HERO

One of these DIFFERENT things would be nice, two better, three swell. It may help if they are fully in mind before tackling the rest.

A different murder method could be—different. Thinking of shooting, knifing, hydro-cyanic, garroting, poison needles, scorpions, a few others, and writing them on paper gets them where they may suggest something. Scorpions and their poison bite? Maybe mosquitoes or flies treated with deadly germs?

If the victims are killed by ordinary methods, but found under strange and identical circumstances each time, it might serve, the reader of course not knowing until the end, that the method of murder is ordinary.

Scribes who have their villain's victims found with butterflies, spiders or bats stamped on them could conceivably be flirting with this gag.

Probably it won't do a lot of good to be too odd, fanciful or grotesque with murder methods.

The different thing for the villain to be after might be something other than jewels, the stolen bank loot, the pearls, or some other old ones.

Here, again one might get too bizarre.

Unique locale? Easy. Selecting one that fits in with the murder method and the treasure—thing that villain wants—makes it simpler, and it's also nice to use a familiar one, a place where you've lived or worked. So many pulpateers don't. It sometimes saves embarrassment to know nearly as much about the locale as the editor, or enough to fool him.

Here's a nifty much used in faking local color. For a story laid in Egypt, say, author finds a book titled "Conversational Egyptian Easily Learned," or something like that. He wants a character to ask in Egyptian, "What's the matter?" He looks in the book and finds, "El khabar, eyh?" To keep the reader from getting dizzy, it's perhaps wise to make it clear in some fashion, just what that means. Occasionally the text will tell this, or someone can repeat it in English. But it's a doubtful move to stop and tell the reader in so many words the English translation.

The writer learns they have palm trees in Egypt. He looks in the book, finds the Egyptian for palm trees, and uses that. This kids editors and readers into thinking he knows something about Egypt.

Here's the second installment of the master plot.

Divide the 6000 word yarn into four 1500 word parts. In each 1500 word part, put the following:

FIRST 1500 WORDS

1–First line, or as near thereto as possible, introduce the hero and swat him with a fistful of trouble. Hint at a mystery, a menace or a problem to be solved–something the hero has to cope with.

2–The hero pitches in to cope with his fistful of trouble. (He tries to fathom the mystery, defeat the menace, or solve the problem.)

3–Introduce ALL the other characters as soon as possible. Bring them on in action.

4–Hero's endeavors land him in an actual physical conflict near the end of the first 1500 words.

5–Near the end of first 1500 words, there is a complete surprise twist in the plot development.

SO FAR:

• Does it have SUSPENSE?

- Is there a MENACE to the hero?

- Does everything happen logically?

At this point, it might help to recall that action should do something besides advance the hero over the scenery. Suppose the hero has learned the dastards of villains have seized somebody named Eloise, who can explain the secret of what is behind all these sinister events. The hero corners villains, they fight, and villains get away. Not so hot.

Hero should accomplish something with his tearing around, if only to rescue Eloise, and surprise! Eloise is a ring-tailed monkey. The hero counts the rings on Eloise's tail, if nothing better comes to mind.

They're not real. The rings are painted there. Why?

SECOND 1500 WORDS

1–Shovel more grief onto the hero.

2–Hero, being heroic, struggles, and his struggles lead up to:

3–Another physical conflict.

4–A surprising plot twist to end the 1500 words.

NOW:

- Does second part have SUSPENSE?

- Does the MENACE grow like a black cloud?

- Is the hero getting it in the neck?

- Is the second part logical?

DON'T TELL ABOUT IT *** Show how the thing looked. This is one of the secrets of writing; never tell the reader–show him. (He trembles, roving eyes, slackened jaw, and such.) MAKE THE READER SEE HIM.

When writing, it helps to get at least one minor surprise to the printed page. It is reasonable to to expect these minor surprises to sort of inveigle the reader into keeping on. They need not be such profound efforts. One method of accomplishing one now and then is to be gently misleading. Hero is examining the murder room. The door behind him begins slowly to open.

He does not see it. He conducts his examination blissfully. Door eases open, wider and wider, until–surprise! The glass pane falls out of the big window across the room. It must have fallen slowly, and air blowing into the room caused the door to open. Then what the heck made the pane fall so slowly? More mystery.

Characterizing a story actor consists of giving him some things which make him stick in the reader's mind. TAG HIM.

BUILD YOUR PLOTS SO THAT ACTION CAN BE CONTINUOUS.

THIRD 1500 WORDS

> 1–Shove| the grief onto the hero.

> 2–Hero makes some headway, and corners the villain or somebody in:

> 3–A physical conflict.

4—A surprising plot twist, in which the hero preferably gets it in the neck bad, to end the 1500 words.

DOES:

- It still have SUSPENSE?

- The MENACE getting blacker?

- The hero finds himself in a hell of a fix?

- It all happens logically?

These outlines or master formulas are only something to make you certain of inserting some physical conflict, and some genuine plot twists, with a little suspense and menace thrown in.

Without them, there is no pulp story.

These physical conflicts in each part might be DIFFERENT, too. If one fight is with fists, that can take care of the pugilism until next the next yarn. Same for poison gas and swords.

There may, naturally, be exceptions. A hero with a peculiar punch, or a quick draw, might use it more than once.

The idea is to avoid monotony.

ACTION:

Vivid, swift, no words wasted. Create suspense, make the reader see and feel the action.

ATMOSPHERE:

Hear, smell, see, feel and taste.

DESCRIPTION:

Trees, wind, scenery and water.

THE SECRET OF ALL WRITING IS TO MAKE EVERY WORD COUNT.

FOURTH 1500 WORDS

1–Shovel the difficulties more thickly upon the hero.

2–Get the hero almost buried in his troubles. (Figuratively, the villain has him prisoner and has him framed for a murder rap; the girl is presumably dead, everything is lost, and the DIFFERENT murder method is about to dispose of the suffering protagonist.)

3–The hero extricates himself using HIS OWN SKILL, training or brawn.

4–The mysteries remaining–one big one held over to this point will help grip interest—are cleared up in course of final conflict as hero takes the situation in hand.

5–Final twist, a big surprise, (This can be the villain turning out to be the unexpected person, having the "Treasure" be a dud, etc.)

6–The snapper, the punch line to end it.

HAS:

- The SUSPENSE held out to the last line?

- The MENACE held out to the last?

- Everything been explained?

- It all happen logically?

- Is the Punch Line enough to leave the reader with that WARM FEELING?

- Did God kill the villain? Or the hero?

Lester Dent (1904 – 1959) was a prolific pulp fiction author of numerous stories, best known as the main author of the series of stories about the superhuman character, "Doc Savage."

Nelson S. Bond

Foolproof Fiction: It's All A Matter of Timing

A FORMULA BY NELSON S. Bond

> *Note: Believed to be in the public domain as* this article comes from the October, 1940 issue of Writer's Digest. The copyright records from 1940 do not show a filing for either the magazine issue or the article itself. Neither is there an entry in 1968, the year it would have needed to be renewed. Found on Storyhack.com

It's the damnedest thing! I stand up there with my heart full of hope and my mitts full of driver; I wiggle and I waggle; I straighten my left arm and lower my head; I haul my hips back. I swing. My clubhead goes swoosh! – and the ball goes ploop! A one hundred and fifty yard drive. Fifty up, fifty down, and fifty yards into the lush tangle of crab grass between the tee and the fairway.

My companion says, "Tsk," and stares after my ball thoughtfully. "You going after it?" she asks. "Be careful. There's lions and tigers in there!"

She takes her stance. She's tiny and slim, and her hands are soft. She weighs 106 in her Kaysers. Her biceps are about as tough and sinewy as a cup custard. She swings. A gentle little swaying motion. But the club head goes splat! against the ball. Said pill takes off like a homing pigeon; soars high and far and true, and comes to rest at long last, gleaming whitely upon the green bosom of the fairway halfway to the pin.

Why? I weigh more than she does. I'm taller. I'm stronger. My clubs are heavier.

IF I WROTE LIKE I GOLF, there wouldn't be any long, lazy, blood-pressure-raising afternoons on the links. There would be handouts and patched breeches and truckloads of rejection slips. But by some quirk of fate-possibly because the gods have a celestial budget to balance-I am so lucky as to possess, in my vocation, that which I can't grasp when I'm playing. A sense of timing.

I'm not sure that I can tell you what it is, or how to do it. I suspect it's One of Those Things, like swimming or swinging a golf club or knowing that the third Scotch-and is enough. You have it or you don't. If you don't, you just keep on plugging, going through the motions, until one day, suddenly, there it is and you know what I'm talking about.

And when you've got it, you're sitting pretty. Meat on the table, checks in the poke, and luh-huv in my heart for yoo-hoo!

You're bound to get it, too, if you keep working at it. You know the old gag about how "every writer has to get a million lousy words out of his system." Of course, that's the old malarkey. Some writers click on the first go-round, others (like myself) have to do it the hard way. The truth remains, though, that those first, feeble, fumbling attempts are valuable. Every word you put on paper is another lesson in writing. Even if the story comes bouncing back with the stamps still moist, you've learned something from it. Maybe you've just learned how not do it next time. And, buddy, if you have-that's valuable!

Did I hear a snarl in the audience? You want me to skip the fight-talk, huh? Get down to business? All right. You're asking for it. Here's my theory on the way to "time" a normal, 5,000 word story in such a way as to make it fast, dramatic and salable.

I don't guarantee it; I don't claim that all other methods are wrong. I believe, with Kipling, that "there are six-and-twenty ways of constructing tribal lays . . . every single one of them is right!" All I say is that this works for me.

DESIGN FOR BRICKLAYING A STORY

(Patent not worth applying for)

General Instructions

LAY OUT APPROXIMATELY 20-25 sheets of clean, white paper. I prefer Corrasable Bond because it actually does-as Arnold Gingrich of Esquire puts it-"take erasure with dignity." And an ordinary pencil eraser, to. If the Eaton People want to send me a check for this plug, I'm not proud. Use the 16, rather than the 20 pound weight. It costs less, and keeps down the postage.

Lay out an equal amount of yellow "second sheets," a piece of carbon paper, your cigarettes and matches – Hold it! Change that typewriter ribbon! Your chances of selling fade in direct proportion to the fading of your ink, friend! Now put that damned thesaurus away. Hide it! If you don't know the words and use them in your ordinary conversation, they'll bulge in your story like an olive in a snake's gut.

We'll take it for granted you know how to title and identify your manuscript. If you don't you shouldn't be reading this; you should be studying back issues of Writer's Digest. Name and address in upper left corner, approximate number of words in upper right, title and your name halfway down the page. All right! Let's go!

First 1000 Words. Ends on Page 5.

GET GOING WITH A BANG! Remember, you're writing a short story, not Gone With the Wind. You can't waste words, nor will the editor permit you to waste his or the readers' time. Your first thousand words must tell who are to be the central characters of this work-of-art, when the story takes place, where the scene is set, what the problem is, and set the question as to how the hero expects to take care of it.

Get me straight! I don't mean you should start off anything like this-

"John Marmaduke Frasier, tall, blonde and handsome Sheriff of Burp's Crossing, Arizona, strode down Main Street wondering what he should do about saving the property of his fiancée, sweet Hildegarde Phlewzy, from the clutches of rich bank president, Phineas Gelt, who threatened to foreclose the mortgage on August 19th, 1904, twenty days hence . . ."

You think I'm crazy, eh? Nobody ever introduced a story that way? Guess again! I sat beside Harry Widmer of Ace Publications for a full hour one afternoon, reading over his shoulder unsolicited manuscripts that opened in exactly that fashion. Needless to say, the stories were not offered by "regulars," nor did they come in the folders of an agent. They were the "unrush" mail, i.e., the free-lance offerings that earn pale blue slips reading, "We regret to say-"

But get the thing moving. Start with something happening to somebody; not with mental maunderings, Grab your hero by the neck and shove him smack into a mess of trouble. Then show who started that trouble-and why. Introduce the other persons involved in the problem, make their opening speeches depict their characters. As you write, keep an eye on your page numbers. Remember that this phase of the story must be finished by the middle of page 5.

End the opening sections with the implication that Our Hero recognizes his difficulty and knows what he's going to do about it.

Second 1000 words. Ends on Page 9-10.

THIS IS THE PHASE WHEREIN Our Hero's star is in the ascendancy. Things move along with reasonable assurance of eventual success. Looks like the problem wasn't so terrible after all. With matters moving smoothly, this section may also be used for brief, telling "flashbacks" (if required), and for strengthening characterizations.

A word about scene changes. Many beginning writers seem to go haywire over time and place transitions. That's simply because they make an easy job tough for themselves. For instance, We've all seen manuscripts in which a character leaves a room, goes to another place, meets other people. The beginner, his "timing" hopelessly off, tries to follow the character all the way-

"He stalked from the building indignantly, found a taxi at the door, rode uptown, got out at his own apartment, paid off the cabby, took the elevator upstairs..."

Sharper-edged, neater and vastly more readable is a device used by all professionals and editors. The bridging of time by a quadruple space. Finish one scene. Slap your space-lever twice-and begin your new section with a scene as fresh, as new, as clean-cut as if you were starting an entirely new story!

Here's the way it works in actual practice. Scene one was in the apartment of a detective, Sid ("Softy") O'Neill. A policeman has come

to bring Softy to headquarters. The first scene ends and the second scene begins as follows.

"Okay, let's go!" (said Softy.) Then he remembered and jerked open a drawer in his desk. Dull blue glinted as he jammed something into a harness beneath his left arm-pit. "Let's go!" he repeated.

The Chief said, "Gentlemen, meet Detective O'Neill. Sid is not a member of the city force, but as I told you . . ."

It is not until some paragraphs later that the Chief is introduced by name, or the second phase of the plot determined. But story stuff is unimportant here; we are concerned only with the question of time-and-place transitions. During the blank space left above, Softy O'Neill presumably covered a number of city miles and consumed a half hour's time. The reader is made conscious of that by implication. You don't have to drag him along the route with you. How Softy got to headquarters is unimportant; all that matters is that he got there! Save words, save time. It's all a matter of timing!

Third 1000 words. Ends on Page 13-15.

HERE'S WHERE THE HERO stubs his toe. Things looked good-now the Villain heaves a monkey wrench onto the woiks! Trouble-with a capital "Boo!"-pops up. Technically this is known as a "plot complication." Which is just a literary way of saying it's a, "Dood Dod, what do I do now?" mess.

Let's backtrack a moment and dovetail this. We'll suppose our story to have been (1) sports, (2) science-fiction, (3) detective, (4) love, (5) romantic adventure. Show how a "complication" piles on the major problem in each of the aforementioned.

1.   Hero flashy player, without his team cannot win

championship vital to athletic future of small college. In phase one, main problem set forth. In phase two, path looks easy-hero going like house afire. Phase three, complication-vital blocking back busts leg before crucial game!

2. Hero hastily finishing spaceship with which to visit Mars; must get special Martian desert weed to stave off dreadful scourge which threatens to destroy Earth. Complication. Enemy scientists corners market on beryllium, vitally essential metal for construction of spaceship.

3. Detective hero hunting Red Jornegan, gangster, whose fingerprints were found all over gun that murdered cop. Tracks Jornegan to hide-out. Complication. Finds Jornegan dead, killer's gun lying across room with Jornegan's fingerprints on it! (Whew! This one came off the top of my mind. I wonder whodunit?)

4. Hero admires movie idol, wangles introduction, succeeds in making him veddy, veddy interested. Soft odor of orange blossoms in distance, and then-complication! Learns his contract has a nix-wedding-bells clause.

5. Hero, Foreign Legion lieutenant, besieged by a mob of howling Bedouins. Must carry news of uprising to post. Remembers cache of ammunition in desert. Finds it. Complication. Bullets are for different rifle!

In short, then, this complication is generally something he did not nor could have possibly expected; it may even be a break the villain himself did not count on. But it makes a helluva situation for Our Hero.

Fourth 1000 words. Ends on Page 17-19.

HEREIN, TWO THINGS happen. The Hero, finds, thinks, or fights his way out of the complication. This consumes almost all of the fourth phase. And when we've suffered with him, bled him into open country again-

Up pops the Villain with his deepest, most dastardly plot, unfolded, finally, in all its dire ramifications!

This is the trouble! Ossa on Pelion, if youse lugs know what I mean. This is the spot wherein (in the ancient mellerdramers) Nick Carter used to get two busted legs and a broken back, while a horde of savages armed with scythes and swords and Stuka bumbers swarmed in on him.

That won't go today-thank heaven! I've heard too much poppycock and balderdash about how "the pulps demand an excess of emotion." Action, yes! True emotion, yes! But in my opinion, they neither want, nor will buy, blatantly overwritten mellerdrama.

Anyway, that's a good rule to go buy. Figure it this way and you can't go far wrong-the only reason pulps print hokey stuff is that sometimes they can't get the smooth kind of writing they'll grab when it's offered to them. Let a man learn his trade, and he'll be snatched up by the slicks in a split-second. I think none of the following ex-pulpateers will object if I mention their names in passing: William R. Cox, who has parlayed his Dime Sport muscle men into American, Liberty, et al. Ernest Haycox, who sells super-Westerns to every top-ranking magazine and to Hollywood. Richard Sale . . . Jacland Marmur . . . William Fay . . . but why go on? Their stories had what it takes; they've moved up (Yeah, yeah, I know, they still sell some to the pulps!) and others can profit by studying their techniques.

Some digression. We were in Phase Four, where Our Hero is up to his neck in Trouble. And the Villain is on the bank, heaving rocks at his head.

How to get him out? That's your problem, pal! If I knew, I'd write the story, not donate the outline. But there are several sturdy, tried-and-true methods. By his superior knowledge. By a quirk of chance carefully planted in the earlier part of the story (none of that long arm of coincidence stuff)! By sheer fighting ability.

And he accomplishes this in—

The Fifth 1000 words. Ends on Page 21-25.

THIS IS THE PHASE OF the solution, of final explanation, of denouement. In the detective story, here's where your cop or shamus explains whodunit, why, and how he figured it out. In the western, science, sport or action story, this is where Our Hero fights free and, tying up loose ends, explains to his public how he knew just what to do.

The fifth phase of begins with violent action, tears along swiftly, leading to a swift, decisive conclusion-and ends happily.

Watch your timing here! Pace your final conflict so that the action of it consumes approximately 500 words or more. Previous action may have been truncated to move the story along-but not this final scene. Your readers have suffered with the Hero for 4,000 words. Give 'em a blow-by-blow description of the Last Stand, let their empathies jump with glee as the Villain flinches, cowers, and dies.

I could mention a half dozen writing "tricks" that arouse this emphatic feeling, but there's no time to do so in this article. Nor is this the proper place to do it. This is simply a blueprint, a method of mechanically plotting the short story, that has worked for me-and it will work for you, if you'll give it a trial.

If you'll hew to the page-markers set forth here, I think you'll have no more trouble with tedious openings, long, drowsy middle sections, stories that refuse to end. Because writing-like that confounded golf swing I cannot master-is all a matter of timing.

Oh, I said that before, didn't I? Well-it still goes!

Michael Moorcock

BY ERIC ROSENFIELD from his blog post:

http://www.wetasphalt.com/content/how-write-book-three-days-lessons-michael-moorcock

In the early days of Michael Moorcock's 50-plus-years career, when he was living paycheck-to-paycheck, he wrote a whole slew of action-adventure sword-and-sorcery novels very, very quickly, including his most famous books about the tortured anti-hero Elric. In 1992, he published a collection of interviews conducted by Colin Greenland called Michael Moorcock: Death is No Obstacle, in which he discusses his writing method. In the first chapter, "Six Days to Save the World", he says those early novels were written in about "three to ten days" each, and outlines exactly how one accomplishes such fast writing.

So all of the quotes below are from just the first chapter of the book.

If you're going to do a piece of work in three days, you have to have everything properly prepared.

[The formula is] The Maltese Falcon. Or the Holy Grail. You use the quest theme, basically. In The Maltese Falcon it's a lot of people after the same thing, which is the Black Bird. In Mort D'Arthur it's also a lot of people after the same thing, which is the Holy Grail. That's the formula for Westerns too: everybody's after the gold of El Dorado or whatever. (Cf the MacGuffin.)

The formula depends on that sense of a human being up against superhuman forces, whether it's Big Business, or politics, or supernatural Evil, or whatever. The hero is fallible in their terms, and doesn't really want to be mixed up with them. He's always just about to walk out when something else comes along that involves him on a personal level. (An example of this is when Elric's wife gets kidnapped.)

There is an event every four pages, for example—and notes. Lists of things you're going to use. Lists of coherent images; coherent to you or generically coherent. You think: 'Right, Stormbringer [a novel in the Elric series]: swords; shields; horns, and so on.

[I prepared] a complete structure. Not a plot, exactly, but a structure where the demands were clear. I knew what narrative problems I had to solve at every point. I then wrote them at white heat; and a lot of it was inspiration: the image I needed would come immediately [when] I needed it. Really, it's just looking around the room, looking at ordinary objects and turning them into what you need. A mirror: a mirror that absorbs the souls of the damned.

You need a list of images that are purely fantastic: deliberate paradoxes, say: the City of Screaming Statues, things like that. You just write a list of them so you've got them there when you need them. Again, they have to cohere, have the right resonances, one with the other.

The imagery comes before the action, because the action's actually unimportant. An object to be obtained—limited time to obtain it. It's easily developed, once you work the structure out.

Time is the important element in any action adventure story. In fact, you get the action and adventure out of the element of time. It's a classic formula: We've only got six days to save the world! Immediately you've set the reader up with a structure: there are only six days, then five, then four and finally, in the classic formula anyway, there's only 26 seconds to save the world! Will they make it in time?

Once you've started, you keep it rolling. You can't afford to have anything stop it.

The whole reason you plan everything beforehand is so that when you hit a snag, a desperate moment, you've actually got something there on your desk that tells you what to do.

I was also planting mysteries that I hadn't explained to myself. The point is, you put in the mystery, it doesn't matter what it is. It may not be the great truth that you're going to reveal at the end of the book. You just think, I'll put this in here because I might need it later.

You start off with a mystery. Every time you reveal a bit of it, you have to do something else to increase it. A good detective story will have the same thing. My God, so that's why Lady Carruthers's butler Jenkins was peering at the keyhole that evening. But where was Mrs. Jenkins?

What I do is divide my total 60,000 words into four sections, 15,000 words apiece, say; then divide each into six chapters. ... In section one the hero will say, There's no way I can save the world in six days unless I start by getting the first object of power. That gives you an immediate goal, and an immediate time element, as well as an overriding time element. With each section divided into six chapters, each chapter must then contain something which will move the action forward and contribute to that immediate goal.

Very often it's something like: attack of the bandits—defeat of the bandits—nothing particularly complex, but it's another way you can achieve recognition: by making the structure of a chapter a miniature of the overall structure of the book, so everything feels coherent. The more you're dealing with incoherence, with chaos, the more you need to underpin everything with simple logic and basic forms that will keep everything tight. Otherwise the thing just starts to spread out into muddle and abstraction.

So you don't have any encounter without information coming out of it. In the simplest form, Elric has a fight and kills somebody, but as they die they tell him who kidnapped his wife. Again, it's a question of economy. Everything has to have a narrative function.

[On The Lester Dent Master Plot Formula] First, he says, split your six-thousand-word story up into four fifteen hundred word parts. Part one, hit your hero with a heap of trouble. Part two, double it. Part three, put him in so much trouble there's no way he could ever possibly get out of it. Then—now this could be Lester Dent or it could be what I learnt when I was on Sexton Blake Library, I forget—you must never have a revelation of something that wasn't already established; so, you couldn't unmask a murderer who wasn't a character established already. All your main characters have to be in the first third. All you main themes and everything else has to be established in the first third, devloped in the second third, and resolved in the last third. (Note: this last sentence is reminiscent of the classic three-act structure.) (Note 2: Lester Dent's Master Plot Formula is actually a bit more complex and specific than this.)

There's always a sidekick to make the responses the hero isn't allowed to make: to get frightened; to add a lighter note; to offset the hero's morbid speeches, and so on.

...

The hero has to supply the narrative dynamic, and therefore can't have any common-sense. Any one of us in those circumstances would say, 'What? Dragons? Demons? You've got to be joking!' The hero has to be driven, and when people are driven, common sense disappears. You don't want your reader to make common sense objections, you want them to go with the drive; but you've got to have somebody around who'll act as a sort of chorus.

'When in doubt, descend into a minor character.' So when you've reached an impasse, and you can't move the action any further with your major character, switch to a minor character 's viewpoint which will allow you to keep the narrative moving and give you time to think.

H. Bedford Jones

The original "King of Pulps" - from his classic: "This Fiction Business"

Rewriting

ONE OF THE VEXED QUESTIONS about this writing game of ours, my brethren, is the rewriting of manuscript. Most authorities advise that a story should be rewritten several times, and cite the example of the masters. Many authors give out sob-interviews regarding their enormous labor on every story produced.

It is interesting to read all this, of course, and to know that an author is painstaking and worn down to the paint of exhaustion by each story. However, being neither an authority nor an author, merely a moderately successful commercial fictionist, I find myself unable to accept the matter as viewed by others, and much prefer my own innocent standpoint and custom. If some of us had to re-write each story before selling it, we would not make money.

Although I seldom practice it, I do believe that re-writing a story once is always a good thing for the story. Here again, it depends hugely upon the individual—upon you yourself. If you are prolific, turning out quick work, it is liable to carelessness; rewriting is the rule for you. If you are slow and painstaking, if every paragraph makes you sweat blood, then re-writing will smooth down your whole manuscript.

If you are an inexperienced writer, however—what then?

Look at the matter logically. You want to earn a living from writing fiction. In order to do so, you must write with some facility—not necessarily quickly, but with facility. You must train your brain to this. I could me half a dozen men who can write a story of any length, on any subject, in any given space of time. Magazines like to depend on such men, very often.

Suppose you take I manuscript, and work on it six months, altering and rewriting. What have you to show when you get through? One story, perhaps good and perhaps not. Have you learned enough to nuke this work worth while? No—emphatically, no!

You have learned a good deal about story writing through this work, no doubt. You have corrected a lot of mistakes, you have produced one fine story. But you have given your brain no facility, and you are so sick of that cursed story you could gladly throw it away.

An alternative frequently proposed, is that you lay aside for several months everything you write, then take it up and re-write it. That is just as bad. You haw lost your enthusiasm about that story, in the interim; you have cooled off. When you take it up, the thing is like a school exercise to you, and hard to rewrite.

This alternative is too extreme altogether, and I have a much better scheme to set forth. It has proven good for me in experience, and wherever used has greatly improved my own work.

When you finish a story, your mind is hot with it; you firmly believe it to he the best short story ever written. Everyone does! Well, then, let it repose in your drawer for a couple of days, and busy yourself with something else entirely different. Then go hack to your story, and give it a complete revision. Your mind is still enthused over it, yet time enough has passed to let you see the mistakes and visualize changes that might improve it. Such is the formula. Let the thing alone for several weeks, and your enthusiasm has grown cold. Work and slave over it, time after time, and you come to hate it

How, you say, does this give the brain facility? Because you are spending less time over one story, and you are turning out more stories. That's what counts—learning by doing—faith by works! By all means give your stories a revision; but give than only one. Make it thorough, honest, laborious. Then, if the tale won't sell, forget it.

Many of us, who have attained facility and got the knack, sell the first draft of a story and it is a completed story. Out of about a hundred booklengths written and sold, I do not believe that ten have received anything more than a revision for mistakes, grammatical errors, and other such "slips." Not one has been actually unwritten. Often a portion of one is rewritten to effect some change in the story, but then only a few pages are affected. It would be much better for our work if it were given more care, I grant you. On short stories it does get more care.

The revision of a story is particularly hard for a novice, because it is hard for him to see when his mistakes lie. The remedy for this, of course, is the professional critic. But how do you know that the critic does not turn over your story to a stenographer, and send you "form letter 6" in criticism? Something of the sort has been done ere this, and will be done again.

There are, I make no doubt, professional critics who give honest criticism; even they are working from theory alone, and from established rules. There are so many of them in the field, however, that I am constrained to think some of them must be excellent. Some of them simply mm: give an honest, individual criticism that is worth something. How to find out who these men are? The best way, is perhaps by experience. Try them out and use your head. Criticize the criticism for yourself, sud let your common sense do the rest.

All this, remember, is nothing but the viewpoint of one men, who does not claim to be an authority, a critic or a figure in literature, and who is merely telling the truth about commercial writing, as he sees it. He my be wrong all the way through. Probably he is wrong I good share of the way. At least, he can write and sell a story, however!

When you are learning to write, you want to learn to *write*—time enough later to learn revision and polishing. To advise a young writer to "ceaselessly polish, revise, polish again" is venerable and absolute bush—utter nonsense! How should an inexperienced writer know how to polish and revise? It is a supremely difficult achievement. Anatole France laid down half a dozen simple rules; I kept them by me a year or two, but the manuscripts on which I used them did not sell very readily, and I discarded his advice. What the young writer needs is a little rewriting, and a very great deal of writing.

Come, then, my weary brethren, and let us be concrete. You need to do all kinds of writing, tackle all sorts of material, before you find the medium best suited to you. No two people make the same errors, or will need the same sort of criticism. You must be your own critic. Make out for yourself A list of mistakes, apply them to each story you write, and then re-write the story just once with the list propped in front of you. Change the wording as much in possible, in order to practice fluency in words. Read the dictionary to enlarge your vocabulary.

But—don't sit down and stew over a story until you hate it. Don't force yourself to a job from which you get no pleasure and into which you can put no enthusiasm. A story is like one of the old Chinese bronzes which were gold-plated in the fire. The finish may not be perfect, but too much rubbing will certainly wear away the gold and leave the bronze.

The story "D'Artagnan," published in *Adventure* and as a book by Covici, Frieda Inc., was only a month in the writing. Except in two or three places, it was not rewritten or revised. It contained one glaring and egregious blunder, which passed the author and the proof readers for both magazine and publishers – and why did it pass them? Because they were all too much interested in fine story at that point. They admitted it.

So think twice before you polish too hard...

Plot

THE WORD "PLOT" IS one of the professional walls raised around the amateur writer. The term is dwelt upon with great unction and ritual. Plot is the all important thing—if he is going to write fiction, then he must strive for plot, plot, plot!

I most disrespectfully submit that this is absolutely B-U-N-K.

In the first place, let us determine just what the word plot means—not an easy thing by a good deal. I do not believe it can be defined more accurately than in the precise words of Pitkin: *"Plot is a climactic series of events, each of which both determines and is determined by the characters involved."* There, in a nutshell, is the clearest definition of plot ever attained.

At the same time, few people entertain the same notion about plot. Poe held that a story had an excellent plot when none of its component parts could be removed without detriment to the whole structure; yet this is far from conveying the exact meaning. Poe's stories had very little plot, as the word is commonly understood among writers today. Therefore, I have actually seen him held up as a bad example in this respect—Poe, who made himself a classic in English, and whom Baudelaire made a classic in French! It is undeniably true, however, that the world's greatest men are usually held up as bad examples.

Howells, on the contrary, believed that any plot was constituted by a series of events which grew entirely out of the central character. This is the literary viewpoint, usually followed by great artists like Howells, and applies chiefly to novels. The didactic viewpoint, that of Pitkin as stated above, is entirely satisfactory, and is the belief held by schools and teachers and by many writers. It is the strict dramatic plot. Read over any good play, and you'll be able to apply Pitkin's definition and to understand it more clearly.

However, we are not dealing with literature or the drama; our interest is centered on the business of fiction—and the foregoing remarks have nothing to do with it. Therefore let us consider the horrible proposition: A Good Story Needs No Plot.

Reflect, brethren! Some of the best short stories ever written have very little, if any, plot. That is why some professors stuffily refuse to call them short stories, and apply other names to them. It is hard for a teacher to see any horizon—his spectacles are too strong. He wants to keep all young writers between two narrow and high walls—that is his business.

Look at magazine fiction. Has it any pretensions, any purpose, other than to entertain the reader? Absolutely none. A fiction magazine shuns in horror all propaganda, religious controversy, and bore-some highbrow effusions. Its business is simply to make its readers forget their troubles and come again for more. When it ceases to be entertaining, it ceases to have any existence.

Very well, then. What is the most entertaining story ever written? What story has brought delight to the most millions of people and has been most widely read? Probably certain Chinese romances would fill the bill, but we are speaking of the western world; therefore, our answer would be: "The Arabian Nights." Out of this collection of tales, the adventures of Sinbad the Sailor are perhaps the best known. They have not only been read for themselves, but have entered into fiction, myth, drama, all over the world. In the most erudite oriental studies, those of Berthold Laufer, you will find Sinbad and his adventures figuring prominently. And these stories have not the least vestige of plot. They are nothing but loosely woven incidents, which are controlled entirely by chance. So much for plot, as an essential.

On the other hand, we must not be blind to the value of plot in its strictest sense. It is highly essential to many forms of writing. To many commercial writers it is a great aid, and some of them depend altogether upon it. At the same time, it is another of those things which you must grasp and understand in order to disregard if you so prefer. It is another of the many walls around the writer, which his imagination may over-leap.

Certain magazines are strong for plot, and most editors assert with pathetic enthusiasm that they must have plot. As a matter of fact, none of them care a hang about it, and any of them will buy a good story without a plot, just as readily as they would buy one with a strong plot. Let me prove my point, brethren, by a little story just between ourselves, which must pass no farther.

Two editors of well-known fiction magazines were holding a lovely lodge of sorrow over me. They would like to use my stuff, but their magazines were famous for having strong and manly plots. Their readers wanted 'em, looked for them. As one editor expressed himself:

"Your stories are well written, but they're nothing except a lot of incidents strung in a row. They haven't a vestige of plot!"

I might have pointed out that the reading public seemed more or less satisfied with my yarns, and that other magazines were not kicking. Instead of argument, I submitted to each of these editors several stories under a pen-name, keeping carefully from sight my own connection with them. They were even typed in a manner entirely different from my own. And what happened? The gentlemen bought them and wrote enthusiastically for more with offers of contracts.

There are two possible explanations for this. One, that the editors themselves had only a vague idea of what they meant by plot, and had in mind merely a certain type of story. This is highly logical. The second explanation is that plot makes no difference whatever to a good and entertaining story. Take your choice, or combine the two.

Never accept the dicta of a magazine as to what it wants; never guide your work so as to make it fall in line with the "requirements" of a magazine. That is, naturally, unless you're engaged in some special line of hack work, as will be touched upon later. Aim only to turn out an excellent product. An editor would publish the Prophecy of Esdras if he thought it would entertain his readers—and is there not one newspaper, indeed, which is running a serial called The Holy Bible?

Without any desire to be critical, I am quite positive that to editors and teachers the word "plot" is merely professional patter—something to teach and talk about. An editor recently gave me the same old line about a story, said it had no plot, and he'd buy it if I'd put some good strong plot into it. I agreed. I changed the name of one character, deleted one word, had the story copied on fresh paper. And what did he do when he read it again? Bought it as being entirely satisfactory. Of course.

Studying plot development, you understand, will not corrupt your morals in any way, and if you're going into the writing game seriously, you must study plot with the rest. However, do not dally with the notion that plot is the one great essential to be mastered, that a good plot will carry off a poor story. Not by a good deal. Plot is really one of the subservient elements to entertaining fiction.

And returning, upon due reflection, to Edgar Allan Poe's theory, I am inclined to appreciate it more fully. He was one of the first of our commercial writers, and he knew his business down to the ground. When the gentlemen who gently scoff at him can turn out stories which will rival his, then by all means let us accept their dicta with reverence. Until then, let your story be so written that not a paragraph of it could be cut out without positive detriment to the whole yarn—and you needn't worry about whether it has plot or not.

If the story is in you, it will come out. And if, in writing it, you do not commit the deadly sin, you have an excellent chance of. selling it.

Appendix:

How to Study Textbooks About Fiction Writing and Emerge With Sanity Intact

IT'S NOT AS BAD AS it's been made out to be, and it isn't as bad as sitting through professorial pontifications and then having to take a test that you have to pass to not repeat the process again.

The simple bottom line:

Get a stack of books and videos, then throw out what doesn't work for you.

and:

You have to test everything you read. For yourself. On your own writing.

I know a great deal about researching, as I've been doing this for years myself. Researching in all sorts of different fields. Recently, I've been studying fiction writing as I'd wrapped up the other studies.

This article is to tell you the quick routes to effective research.

Surviving Tons of Really Bad Advice

WE TOUCHED ON IT ABOVE.

You are going to be studying writing for the rest of this existence. Because you want to constantly improve. That's in order to help your readers have a better experience and buy more of your books. That in turn improves your author income.

An ideal would be to pile up a stack of books and videos about the subject.

- Now, take out anything in those stacks that have Grammar in the subject or the title.

- Next, take out anything written by a professor or someone in a university.

- Next to remove are anything with scammy titles like Internet Marketers use, such as 'how much money you can make' or 'how easy it is to _____ in just __ steps.' Especially if it has money in the title.

- Some of the better books in this area are written by professional authors who have been publishing bestsellers for decades. (Writer's Digest has a nice series of these.)

- Throw out anything about how to publish books or how to write proposals. That's another study you'll need to do, or already have. Those don't talk primarily about craft, which is your goal..

Also include any online videos from courses you can take in this area. Again, don't buy into the spammy titles from wannabe's. Any teacher is only as good as what they've written – those who have published more non-fiction books on fiction writing than actual fiction are wannabe's. But you'll be able to tell early on, since they mostly talk about how to publish, not how to craft a story.

And don't forget the classic write-ups from Poe, Stephenson, and Bierce. Their prose is somewhat archaic now, but they were successful in their time. A. A. Milne has a few essays on this, as well as "On

Writing" by Stephen King. Best classic I recommend is "Becoming a Writer" by Dorothea Brande.

The main caveats are to stay away from anyone who says there is only one way to do things, or quote authorities or "scientific" studies saying how their advice works.

There Are No Hard And Fast Rules to Fiction Writing

THERE IS ONLY REALLY *what you love to read, what you love to write,* and *what your readers love to buy from you.* If your fiction writing fits in all these categories, then you should be able to make income from it.

What works is what you test for yourself. If it helps you write better and faster, then it's useful. Keep it. Note it down somewhere if you need to. Get it internalized so you don't have to. Make it second-nature.

And that means you are going to have to let go of most of your English classes and training. As I said above, Grammar has nothing to do with writing and you should leave it alone. Even Strunk. His book is good for non-fiction writing, mostly. But not fiction.

Pick up some Patterson fiction or any other consistently bestselling thriller author and look over their sentences. They aren't always. But you can find some arcane Grammar rules which explain them. (A one word sentence can be called an "expressed thought" FWIW.) But you'll take months sleuthing these rules out that you could have spent simply writing.

The best advice I've ever seen or heard is to *write like you talk.* Read your stuff out loud and correct it if you stumble over phrases or run out of breath before you get to the end of an overlong sentence (like this one.)

ProWritingAid.com is a great tool you can use to edit your sentences. They can help you find "sticky" sentences and get rid of pesky adverbs. Also, if you start out with the same word many times.

Learning by Reading

THEN SET UP ANOTHER stack of books, with the authors you really like to read. Also include DVD's of movies and TV shows you've loved to watch. (Ideally, you'd get books they were based on as well.)

This second pile is where most of your real learning will take place.

You have to develop the habit of prolific reading and prolific writing. Every. Single. Day.

You set up some time for reading (like instead of watching mind-numbing genre-TV shows.)

And you set up some time for writing.

Maybe with your day job and your commutes, you aren't left with much time after you fix your meals and help the kids with their homework. One author with three small kids would write in 30 minute sprints, whenever he could get the time. Another housewife wrote when the kids left for school and until they came back. Another author got up and went to work an hour early to get his writing done before the day started. Yet another had daily commutes on the train, and so took his laptop and headphones so he could write both ways.

Set the time and do the writing. Brande has some great ideas down this line in her book.

Only read what you love. If the book you are reading is difficult and you want to set it down, go ahead and do just that. The books that take you right to the end and you want more by that author and about that character – *those* are the ones you want to study.

Brande says to read that great book once, then take notes about what stood out for you about it, and then go back through the book looking for how that author made that happen.

Look over the sentences, the word choice, the length of paragraphs, the length of chapters, all that sort of stuff. This is where you'll build your vocabulary and get ideas.

You can also dissect each chapter for openings, major incidents, and endings. Do that for a whole book and you'll get some ideas about how to plot. You'll learn more by dissection than you will by reading books about plotting theory. Because the examples you read (or even watch as movies) and enjoy are the ones you want to study and learn from. They are doing something right for you.

The One Key Idea – Test This For Yourself

"DOES EACH STORY I READ help me write better or faster?"

That's the key point.

In general, I am a bit leery of advice coming from people who sell services to authors. Freelance editors and proofreaders who are pushing their own books and services aren't as trustworthy as an ebook you can get for under ten bucks and delete if it doesn't work.

I've bought more than one course which I didn't open again after I got through it, even though I downloaded all their videos so I would watch them any time I wanted. And I just started reviewing all those courses again recently, and noticed that fact. The investment I made didn't really pay off as much as I wanted.

To be sure, I did usually get major ideas from some of them. Those ideas were not from the courses, but from testing their concepts against the real world and finding something even more major or basic than what they taught.

Until recently, I didn't get any courses in creative writing. I'd only gotten courses in how to publish. Most of the over-hyped books are not about writing, but the mental game of getting yourself to write. The worst course I've seen offered recently said nothing in its promotion about how to write better fiction, but how they would hold your hand for 90 days to ensure you did end up writing and publishing that book. (For a small, today-only discounted price of $2,000.00!)

That's just nuts-and-bolts. Mechanics.

The truly sad point is that you can get all the core data from these "guru's" just out of their free ebooks, free webinars and introductory videos. (And you only have to watch webinars about half-way through, as the rest is a sales pitch.) Taking their courses just spread the same data out over hours and hours.

One huge course said two things of value: Amazon was a search engine, and you had to publish every 30 days to keep your books visible. Funny enough, a free intro course by this same person told where he got the ideas from – and gave he name of that other author's book. (Looking up that other author's blog gave me another source of good data.)

Again, these courses are all about _how-to's_.

I did go through one author's set of courses on writing craft. Right up to the point where not only wasn't I learning anything new, but I was finding that his opinions were getting in the way of finding what really worked. After that, I weeded through those two stacks of books.

We all teach ourselves best by doing. Learn an idea, then write a bunch of stories that test that idea.

By the end of those stories, you'll find that you are either writing faster or better, or both – or not.

If you want to improve your openings, write a few dozen books and concentrate on their openings. Endings (cliff-hangers) are learned by concentrating on reading writers that won't let you go at the end of chapters, and then practicing what makes a good cliffhanger.

Test everything. Starting with what I'm telling you right now.

Some More Ideas to Test For Yourself

1. Write short fiction and short stories to start with.
2. Learn to make these add up into longer works, as serials in a series that can be an anthology.
3. That means you need to study short fiction and short stories from the top bestselling writers. And long-running TV series.
4. Publish weekly, not weakly.

THE IDEA BEHIND THIS is test each advice with short stories that you can write in a few hours.

The worst advice I've heard of will keep a writer slogging away at their first and only novel for years. *Years.*

If you can write 2,000 or better words per day (what Stephen King recommended in his "On Writing") then you can have a short story out in a couple of days. A 20K novella out in 10 days. A 60K novel out in a month. Of course, you'll have to add time in to self-edit, line-edit, and proof. Plus time getting the cover and description as part of publishing.

Regardless, you write the best you can and your speed will pick up as your confidence does.

With short fiction and short stories, this is possible. And by doing this, you can test both your writing abilities and the genre/category you are targeting.

Note: none of these four steps tell you how to write better. They only give you the structure so you can test data on how to improve your writing simply, easily, quickly.

What I Learned from Studying 227 Craft Textbooks

Mostly that I already knew what I needed to know, and that textbook studies don't replace your own reading and a lot of practice by actually writing.

I WENT OUT TO STUDY the highly recommended books out there about How to Write a Damn Good (Fiction) Book – and threw away 95% of them.

That said, I did find some gold nuggets:

- Becoming a Writer – Dorothea Brande

- On Writing – Stephen King

- The Complete Plotto – William Wallace Cook

- Writing to the Point – Algis Budrys

- Characters & Viewpoint – Orson Scott Card

- Conflict, Action & Suspense – William Noble

- Shoot Your Novel – C. S. Lakin

- Writing Popular Fiction – Dean Koontz

- Zen in the Art of Writing – Ray Bradbury

- 20 Master Plots – and How to Build Them – Ronald B. Tobias

The main point with this list of books is that they mostly don't overlap. The other 217 books mostly or completely did. I'm still saving a dozen or so which are specifically about certain genres. But I'll crack those after I have a few dozen of those-type genre fiction books already read and digested and can see what I like.

These are all craft books, not how-to books. There are tons of books out there on self-publishing and getting agents and contracts. Read those if you need to, but the first advice I ever ran across in self-publishing success was to "Write A Damn Good Book." from JA Konrath. Since none of the books talked about this for fiction authors, I had to pile up this stack and go through them.

This list above, and this short chapter now tells you the path to train yourself into that success.

The tricks are few in this:

1. **Write a lot.** (And publish everything.)

2. **Read (Watch) a lot.** (And only what you really like.)

3. **Enjoy what you're writing**, or your readers won't enjoy reading it.

All you really need to know about plotting is in the second chapter of Budry's book. The rest is your PHD – piled higher and deeper. (Cook's best contribution is in his explanation of how plots work. The rest of his massive "Plotto" is just the cherry on top.)

The funniest thing is that most of the top writers out of this list turned out to be "pantzers". But they didn't call themselves that. They said they were writers. (Not re-writers.) And wrote between a thousand and two thousand words per day. Every day. And once they finished, they started their next one.

You won't find editors on this list, or professional proofreaders. There's probably not any professor or academic anything in that list. Some do coaching on the side. Bradbury used to give local college lectures twice a year, but not for a living. Budrys used to teach writers and he was the exception. You'll see when you read his book. Completely non-academic.

How to Weed Out a List of Books

THE REASON FOR THIS was to see what what out there. I got lists of books and scrounged those books here and there. Bought as many as I had to. Big stack of books. Big.

The first point was finding that the pro writers, who have decades of experience, gave the best advice.

But just because a person has written 75 novels, doesn't mean much if they are also holding an Academic position. Wedged in with these were the people who were just collating the conventional wisdom and regurgitating it. You could tell these by how many of the "proper" terms they used in describing various writing viewpoints existed. Thick prose. Useless data.

Below that were the sheer volume of people who came up with their own terms to describe the same things everyone else was covering. Their own twist. But they were just repeating stuff without really improving on anything. Some of these were specialized for screen-writing, and I had to skip them as they weren't covering basics, but special tricks and strategies for getting your screenplay accepted and paid for.

At the very bottom were "texts" on how to write fast and cheap and get people to actually buy it (like they just did to you.)

How to Learn Your Author Craft

1. Only read what you like. But read a lot. (Watching lots of good movies also works.)

2. That will give you examples and ideas of how to write best. And train your unconscious mind.

3. Trust your unconscious mind to give you a good story. Then coordinate this with your conscious mind to get the best story out of it.

4. Write every day. Publish at least every week – something.

5. Once you have your first hundred short stories published, it will get easier. (Eat your elephant one bite at a time.)

6. Every "great" author starts writing genre fiction first. And a lot of writers never become "great", but have a great time and make a decent living. (I've done that with my non-fiction self-publishing, which financed this grand experiment.)

What I Learned From This Process

• Alfred Hitchcock said something like: "A story is just like life, but with the dull bits left out." And that is all there is to writing. "Leave out the stuff that will bore readers." – Elmore Leonard said something like that, too.

• There's one plot: a character strives to find happiness. There is one overall structure. This is in Budrys' seven points (or five, or nine, depending on how you count them.) And you have Lester Dent's model, plus Joseph Campbell's

Monomyth. They all fit into each other. They all say the same thing.

• People read to identify with a larger-than-life character with larger-than-life attitudes, problems, solutions, and drives. Readers want to be transported. And kept there.

• There are only two types of things you put into books: those things which forward the action (to solve the character's problem) or deepen our understanding of the character(s). You write what readers expect. The best you can. And even better with your next story.

• Beats build into scenes, build into chapters, build into complete stories. (See Lakin's book.)

• A beat, scene, chapter, and all stories only need to be as long as they need to be. The story will tell you. If you're forcing it, then you wrote past the ending. Back up, find it, then delete everything after that.

• You start off by writing short stories, and these eventually will become collections or novels. Depends. On how you write them. Publish everything. (Use pen names to avoid embarrassment.)

• There's no such thing as Writer's Block. You just have to learn to empty your head so you have space for a story to come in. Then write it as best you can. (See Brande's book on that.)

• Don't listen to reviews or critics. (Except maybe-sometimes the 3-stars.) Take all criticism with a grain of salt. ("Those who can't write, become critics.") You're already writing every story better than your last. And you always will. Free advice (criticism, reviews) is like a belly button. Everyone has one, and they aren't all pretty.

• Keep improving your craft by studying only the best. If you don't like what you're reading, no matter who's name is on the cover, then put it aside. Read what you like. Like what you write. Only. Writing is endless joy. If it isn't, start from the top of this and restudy everything.

How to Throw Away Perfectly Rotten Books

USE YOUR EDITOR MIND. If they don't grab you in the first 5 pages or so, dump them.

This is what I learned again last night. Crappy fiction doesn't get any better. Lousy openings don't make a book better. You aren't mining for raw material here. You don't have to be patient. Remember Sturgeon's Law: 90% of all that out there is crud/crap.

I've suffered through collections of short stories until I got disgusted. If I could, I would have thrown that book across the room. But it was on a tablet, so I just deleted if off the device. I wanted to study the tropes of a paranormal sub-genre (werewolves) as I am in the middle of writing about some (you'd have to ask my muse why...). But the editing was a bunch of crap. They through a ton of various and assorted stories and styles and structures. They put tragedies right next to successes. And I put it down more than once. But my mistake was not throwing it away after the first put-down. Because it was crud.

Great books will snag you at the beginning and drag you straight through. Like Louis L'Amour – you can only take a break in the middle of a chapter. (So I'm hunting up his collections of short stories.)

You'll find that they narrow down to certain areas – like the Writer's Digest series "Elements of Fiction Writing". These tend to be more "non-crud" than the rest of my stack.

Resources

Did You Find the Strange Secret in This Book?

ALL OUR BOOKS REFERENCE a strange secret. In their own words.

With complete certainty, I can tell you now – from my more than half-century of existence:

- Any and all of my successes, as well as all my disappointments are directly traced to the principles in this book I want to give you.

- For any set-back or failure, I either didn't know these principles, didn't understand their power, or simply ignored them.

- For every success, I have tracked back to taking these exact steps laid out in this book - to achieve, acquire, or attain whatever it was I wanted to be or have.

And that experience is why I produced this short book you can have - to carry with you and review regularly.

You may have heard about it:

"The Strangest Secret Collection" inspired by the works of Earl Nightingale.

THIS COLLECTION CONTAINS "The Strangest Secret" transcript by Earl Nightingale, plus selections from other related books.

Limited Time Offer

YOU CAN DOWNLOAD YOUR own copy of this book –

as long as its still available.

Visit: https://gum.co/SSC-Giveaway

Related Books You May Like

ALL OUR LATEST RELEASES[1]

Both fiction and non-fiction – each with links to major online book outlets as well as author discounts.

Modern Parables[2]

Our short stories and anthologies – all in order of most recent release.

Classic Fiction[3]

Our ever-expanding collection of fiction stories that are hard to find, yet their stories never grow old. Perfect entertainment when the too-modern world becomes stale...

The Strangest Secret Library[4]

All the full references mentioned in Earl Nightingale's Strangest Secret Library available for instant download – through your online book outlet of choice or with our publisher's discount.

Publishing[5]

Our collection of modern and classic references on how to improve your writing in our modern self-publishing age.

Books on Success and Goal Achievement[6]

---

1. https://livingsensical.gumroad.com/?sort=newest

2. https://livingsensical.gumroad.com/?sort=newest&tags=fiction

3. https://livingsensical.gumroad.com/?query=golden%20age&sort=page_layout

4. https://livingsensical.gumroad.com/?query=strangest%20secret&sort=page_layout

5. https://livingsensical.gumroad.com/?query=publishing&sort=page_layout

6. https://livingsensical.gumroad.com/?query=success&sort=page_layout

Our collection of modern and classic references on how you can become a personal success and achieve your own goals – to get everything you want out of life.

———————————

Visit https://store.livingsensical.com/ to find the book you're looking for

Libraries of Interest

Our No-Cost Libraries

OVER THE YEARS, WE'VE aggregated several top-selling books that people find useful. And mainly, the books we have fit into a handful of categories. For your use, we've built these into libraries, which are all no-charge sign-ups to access PDF versions of these top-selling books:

1. Completely Change Your Life Library:

https://livingsensical.gumroad.com/l/ChangeYourLifeLibrary

(Goal Achievement)

You can have and be anything you want. You can get everything you want out of life. In this library are the tips and tricks to make it all happen for you.

2. Becoming a Writer Library:

https://livingsensical.gumroad.com/l/BecomingAWriterLibrary [7]

(Writing Craft)

There are time-tested and proven methods of writing that leave you refreshed at the end of your writing day – or whatever time you have for it. Writing can be simple, a joy, and bring you peace...

3. Breakthrough Advertising Library:

https://livingsensical.gumroad.com/l/BecomingAWriterLibrary
(Copywriting)

---

7. https://livingsensical.gumroad.com/l/BecomingAWriterLibrary

When you know how people want to be talked to, your ads can help them find the products or services they want. Helping people live better lives isn't full of gimmicky sales tricks. Just stuff that works.

4. Regenerative Agriculture Library:

https://livingsensical.gumroad.com/l/RationalGrazingLibrary (Regenerative Agriculture)

Farming can improve the soil while it supports the families that tend it. It can raise more produce if you plant, graze, and harvest with Nature's proven principles.

5. The Insiders Club:

https://livingsensical.gumroad.com/l/InsidersClub

(Fiction Readers)

For loyal fans – get inside scoops on how these books were written, advance copies for review, and become First Readers – who hear about the stories as they are created. Plus, full Book Universe Notes to get more out of each of our books. For insiders only.

———————

ALL THESE LIBRARIES are live and no-cost to join. Each has around a half-dozen or more of our top-selling books (as PDF's) are in each of these areas for you. Sign up for the ones you want. Simple entertainment or how to fix things in problem areas.

Sign Up Now.

Don't Miss Out!

Want to keep up to date with this author and all upcoming books?

Find out about special discounts?

Hear about pre-release specials, new audiobooks and courses?!?

Instant Access – Join Here

Visit: **https://livingsensical.gumroad.com/l/InsidersClub**

Did You Like This Book?

HOW ABOUT LEAVING A review with the vendor?

Otherwise (or in addition) you can leave your recommendations on:

- Bookbub[8] (https://www.bookbub.com/recommendations)

The whole point is to enable others to find books that you liked reading.

Which then helps you find more great books to read.

And...

Feel free to share this book!

---

8. https://www.bookbub.com/recommendations

Did you love *Learning from the Pulp Masters: 2nd Edition*? Then you should read *How I Survived My First Year of Fiction Writing*[9] by Dr. Robert C. Worstell!

Writing Fiction isn't very hard - *if you throw out 95% of what you've been taught is true.*

Academics and those who earn their income marketing how-to books and courses, as well as freelance editors, proofreaders, and cover designers all have a vested interest in making it seem that writing and publishing is very difficult.

It's just not true at all.

Yes, there is a lot of hard work to it. And it's not something you can learn overnight. And you have to keep studying and practicing your craft to get any good at it - just as musicians and athletes practice daily.

---

9. https://books2read.com/u/bO6EyW

10. https://books2read.com/u/bO6EyW

But you can publish your first book on Amazon in a half hour from now. It's that simple. (Of course you can use a pen name to avoid being embarassed later.)

The point is that writing and publishing is simple, and inexpensive.

Here's the secret: **Write short and narrow, publish long and wide.**

Write short stories for a specific sub-genre you like to read.

Publish long in advance (pre-schedule) and wide to every possible outlet - including free ones like Wattpad and Medium.

Including setting up all the accounts, you can publish everywhere on the globe in an afternoon. For no cost, except your time.

This book is a compilation of the blog posts I wrote and published while I was busy doing a test of everything I'd rounded up and studied about writing and publishing fiction.

And it's a very raw, passionate description of exactly what I found works - as I was testing it.

So it's more an adventure that starts from having no published fiction and ends up with have well over a hundred books published. Step by step, blow by blow.

To test what I'd found and bring it all to you.

Scroll Up and Get Your Copy Now.

Read   more   at https://store.livingsensical.com/?query=worstell&sort=page_layout.

Also by Dr. Robert C. Worstell

Becoming A Writer
Dorothea Brande's Becoming A Writer Collection
PLOTTO Genie: The Endless Story

Change Your Life
How to Completely Change Your Life in 30 Seconds, Second Edition

Change Your Life Toolset
Get Your Self Scam Free

Make Yourself Great Again Library
Why You Got All That Stuff
The Art of Wonk, Compleat

Masters of Copywriting
Breakthrough Copywriter 2.0: An Advertising Field Guide to Eugene
M. Schwartz' Classic

Claude C. Hopkins' Scientific Advertising With My Life in Advertising

Mindset Stacking Guides
Make Yourself Great Again Part 1
Make Yourself Great Again Part 2
Make Yourself Great Again Part 3
Make Yourself Great Again Part 4
Choose. Believe. Win.
Make Yourself Great Again - Complete Collection
Go Thunk Yourself, Again!
The Strangest Secret Collection 2.0
Think Less and Grow Richer
Freedom Is (Period.) 2.0
Seek and Find

PMA Science of Success
Napoleon Hill's PMA: Science of Success Course - An Introduction

Really Simple Writing & Publishing
How To Write And Publish For Free
Backwards Book Publishing: Save Time, Earn More, Work Less
Writing-Publishing Survival Guide
Author Freedom Guidebook
How to Stop Feeding the Beast
How I Survived My First Year of Fiction Writing
Learning from the Pulp Masters: 2nd Edition
How to Become an Instant Author in 30 Seconds

Becoming a Wealthy Writer
Marketers & Writers - Scammers & Dupes
How to Write Less and Profit More - Version 2.0
Writing Serial Fiction In the Real World 2.0

Regenerative Agriculture
Grass Productivity: Rational Grazing, Second Edition

Thrive Learning Life Improvement
Avoiding Online Dating Pitfalls

Standalone
Farm Less, Profit More: Lessons in Regenerative Grazing

Watch for more at
https://store.livingsensical.com/?query=worstell&sort=page_layout.

Midwest Journal Press
Finding You Books that Continue to Change Your Life

About the Publisher

"Finding you books that continue to change your life."

A veteran publishing imprint and a practical philosophy for life, Midwest Journal Press has been active publishing new and established authors since 2006.

We take advantage of the new Print on Demand and ebook technologies to enable wider discovery for authors.

We publish in most of the major genres of fiction and non-fiction.

Our current emphasis is in speculative fiction modern parables.

Find out about our new releases, publisher discounts, and special offers...

Sign Up Now:
http://store.livingsensical.com/follow